SEVEN DAYS WITH A WITCH

By Don Allen

© 2016 Don Allen. All rights reserved. This book or parts thereof may not be reproduced in any form, stored in any retrieval system, or transmitted in any form by any means—electronic, mechanical, photocopy, recording, or otherwise—without prior written permission of the publisher, except as provided by United States of America copyright law. For permission requests, write to the publisher, at "Attention: Permissions Coordinator," at the address below.

Published by DRW PUBLISHING HOUSE

Printed in the United States of America.

Table of Contents

1. Chapter 1   Day 1
2. Chapter 2   Day 2
3. Chapter 3   Day 3
4. Chapter 4   Day 4
5. Chapter 5   Day 5
6. Chapter 6   Day 6
7. Chapter 7   Day 7
8. Chapter 8   Post Chetopa
9. Chapter 9   Back Home
10. Chapter 10   Conclusion

CHAPTER 1

DAY 1

Day 1

The date was September 28, 2014. The events that I am about to share with you changed my life forever. I was invited to hold a tent revival in Chetopa, Kansas, a small town of maybe one-thousand people. It's a farming town off the last Missouri exit on Interstate 44 before you cross the border into Oklahoma, about 45 minutes south of Joplin, Missouri. It's located in the four corners region, where Missouri, Arkansas, Oklahoma and Kansas all meet. No reason to move there. Most everyone there…born there.

Pastor Ray, pastor of the Faith Baptist Church, had contacted me previously in 2011 to come and hold a revival at his church. At that meeting, we had a great revival. Folks came from as far away as Oklahoma City. At that time, the town was doing pretty well. It looked like any other small town—local businesses all along Main Street, with a handful of local churches.

Three years later, in the fall of 2014, I was asked to come and hold a second revival in Chetopa. Pastor Ray wanted to see if he could get more of the community involved if the meetings were held in a tent rather than a church building. On this ministry trip, I felt led to have a few people come with me to help at this revival which, at the time, didn't make any sense to me because it's such a small town. I had on many occasions ministered in much larger venues without a team. Yet, something kept at me, and so I invited Kirk and Angela DeMars, and TJ Whetstone to join me. TJ is Pastor Ray's daughter. She had been helping me with my weekly meetings in the Capitol building in Jefferson City along with Kirk and Angela.

When we rolled into Chetopa, everything seemed different this time. It seemed dark and dead. Right as you cross the little bridge to come into town on Main Street, you could see that the place was almost abandoned. All the homes seemed empty. I would say that seventy-five percent of the businesses that were open just three years prior were closed. There were two gas stations, one as you entered town and one as you left as well as two restaurants, one local grocery store, a few junk shops, and a Farm and Home type business. A few churches had even closed. Little did we know that we would find out exactly why. Chetopa, Kansas had become run down and empty, but more than that, it was just dark. The houses were paint-peeled, the windows broken out. Even the trees looked twisted.

We came into the first night ready to have a great service. There was a core group of people there, not bad for a Sunday night in a community of one-thousand or so. It was good to see that some friends of mine, a Mennonite family we had ministered to who had left the Mennonite church, looking for more of God. They brought some of their children and were going to stay the whole week and camp outside the tent.

We turned on the lights. The praise and worship began. People were standing and singing, "We're going to have a great revival..." The chairs were set up in a half-circle style, surrounding the small stage. I was seated to the right side of the tent on the front row. As I listened to the old hymns and looked over my notes, suddenly, all of that was interrupted.

Have you ever had that feeling that someone is looking at you? That's what I felt. I looked up, scanning the tent, trying to see why I was feeling this way. That's when I first saw her—Angelique.

This woman, accompanied by a man, was just taking her seat all the way on the opposite side of the tent. At first glance, it didn't take a spiritual giant to realize she had problems. You could see that, and I thought, "Well good, she is in the right place and God will touch her tonight."

Still not perceiving who was looking at me, I continued looking at my Bible. Suddenly, the hair stood up on the back of my neck. There was that feeling again, but this time, it was stronger. I looked up again, and this time, there was no guessing. This woman stared directly at me from across that tent. Our eyes met for a moment. I smiled a little, thinking that I just caught her looking at me, but she didn't smile. As a matter of fact, she continued to stare at me with this look of anger. She began to slump down in her chair. It reminded me of when a lion crouches right before it springs on its prey. She hunkered down and never lost eye contact with me until her eyes rolled back into her head, and she passed out.

I looked back down at my Bible, and I'm not going to lie, I was a little freaked out. My mind was racing, "Did anyone else see that? Nope...everyone is enjoying the music." Suddenly, she snapped awake and sat straight up with her eyes locked on mine. She crouched like a lioness until she again passed out. This cycle would repeat itself one more time before I went forward to preach.

Pastor Ray spoke briefly and introduced me to speak. There she was, about four rows back. The whole time I was ministering, she had locked onto me. Now I was close enough to see that there was absolutely no white in her eyes—two fully darkened circles in her head—and she was locked on me!

I continued ministering until I had enough of the threatening demeanor and the woman's oppression. I stopped and said, "We are going to minister to some people now." I looked directly at her and said, "You! Get up here right now!" She began to squirm and twist. I said, "Right now, get up here!" I then called Kirk, Angela and TJ forward to help me pray. She approached us, a very intimidating figure, about 6 feet tall and probably weighed two-hundred thirty pounds. And that *look*. Those eyes...no white....fully blacked out, a case of total possession.

She stumbled forward to the front, and I stood in front of her. TJ stood on one side, Angela to the other, and Kirk behind her. I grabbed her hands and said, "Look at me." She fought the command and began growling—a very low, unsettling growl—one that vibrated my insides. She began to twist in a way that the human body cannot twist. I again said firmly, but very calmly, "Look at me." With everything within fighting her, she looked up. I said, "God loves you." She went into full growling, twisting and shaking, and this voice from way down said,

"Nooooo..."

I said, "Look at me. Look at me. God loves you."

With that other worldly voice, she said "Noooo! Nooo!"

"Look up here. Hold onto my hands. Look up here. God loves you."

"I'm a witch."

I said, "That's ok, God loves you."

Then followed more growling and some explicatives that would not be in good taste to repeat.

"Hey...God loves you."

Kirk, Angela, TJ and I were then joined by two teenage Mennonite girls in praying for her. The fearlessness of the two teenage girls gripped my soul. They weren't scared or intimidated by anything. The woman continued screaming:

"I'm going to pass out. It's killing me! It's killing me! I'm going to die! It's killing me! They are going to kill me. The demons are killing me! I'm going to be sick."

I said, "That's ok, you aren't going anywhere."

We rebuked the demons again, very calmly. There was a peace about this whole process that was truly beyond all understanding. I never raised my voice, yelled or had to get angry. I simply rebuked the demons and continued saying, "God loves you."

Once again we locked eyes. I watched as her eyes would switch back and forth, from solid black to normal, then solid black again. I was speaking to the demon and then to Angelique. The poor woman was clearly being tortured during the battle. The enemy did not want to release her. This went on for a while. I continued to reaffirm God's love for her.

Finally after some time, I said "That's enough." I knew the demons had departed. Later, I asked God how exactly this deliverance worked. I hadn't cast out the demons. I didn't ask them who they were; I didn't bind and loose. All I felt compelled to express was that God loved her over and over again. The Lord said to me, "Truth makes people free. She had been lied to her whole life, having been told that I didn't love her and that I was her enemy. You spoke the truth, and it made her free."

This was her root problem. She never knew love. Everything else was fruit of the root problem. Attack the root, and the fruit will change.

And ye shall know the truth, and the truth shall make you free.

—(John 8:32 KJV)

Once I could see that she was free from demonic control, we led her to the Lord. She accepted Jesus Christ as her Lord and Savior. We didn't know much about her story yet. She had mentioned that she was a witch, but we were focused on the fact that she was free. She went out of the tent, threw up, and returned.

We continued to visit with her, but found it difficult to understand her. Her voice was deep and gravelly. Many times we had to ask her to repeat herself. She finally explained to us that in 2011, she was in the Joplin tornado. She and her husband had been doing meth all day, and he was passed out in the upstairs bedroom. The sirens went off, and like most people that day, she didn't pay too much attention to it. I lived just outside of Joplin at that time, and the sirens had gone off a few times that week already. She was watching TV when the warnings came, and before she knew it, the tornado was upon them. She didn't have any time to try and save him. It destroyed their house, but she lived. They found her husband with his head almost completely severed from his body. She said it was at that moment that a murderous spirit entered her body.

A few days later, Angelique tried to slit her own throat. This is why she was unable to talk. The scar tissue had caused some problems. She lost her children at that time and said she went full blown into Satanism. She was already involved, but this sealed the deal. She no longer cared about anyone or anything. She believed that God was responsible and was consequently her enemy. "*He did this.*" This is when that murderous spirit entered into her.

We ministered to her, reassuring her that God loved her and that he forgave her. I was really just asking her to trust me at that point. She had no idea who God was, but she recognized the power in me and that it came from Him. We made an instant connection at that point. Something supernatural had taken place, and I knew we were in for something amazing.

I continued visiting with Angelique and tried to pry for a bit more info about the whole witch thing. Kirk, Angela and some of the others finished up ministering to the sick that night. Angelique shared with me that she was the High Witch of the Four Corners. I asked her what that meant, but she didn't want to share too much at that time, other than to tell me that this was way more serious than I knew. She did explain, however, that she was appointed to rule over the four state region of Missouri, Oklahoma, Kansas and Arkansas, and that *they* (her family) would not be happy. She went on to hesitantly share with me how she was sent to kill me and the others that were with me that night. She did not share with me how exactly she was going to do that, but she assured me, she was sent to the meeting on an assignment. Angelique said that she was responsible to get the job done and that *they* were not going to be happy that she had failed to carry out her task. She said that she was very scared and kept looking around like someone was after her.

At a later date, Angelique shared with me that she was her coven's "Hit Girl". She was the one they would send to take people out. She shared with me that she had killed three people by physically slitting their throats. I never was able to confirm that, but had no reason to doubt her. Her "Hit Girl" status was confirmed when, later in the week, Angelique and I walked into a church. A grown woman saw her and ran and hid behind Kirk and said, "Please tell Angelique to remove the hit off of my cousin, please!"

That evening, Angelique went home with a Christian lady. She had been previously living with a man who had been trying to help the best that he could. Kirk, Angela, and I went back to the little guest home that the church used for guest ministers to stay in. It was out in the middle of an isolated, dark field. It was creepy for sure. That night, as we prepared for bed, we prayed and talked around the table. I shared with the rest of the team what Angelique had shared with me about being sent to kill us and end the revival in her town. This was an introduction to what the rest of the week was going to be like. None of us could have anticipated the events of that evening or the things that would follow.

We were excited as we realized the magnitude of what had just taken place. As I was lying in bed, I knew they were coming that night. Everything in my flesh crawled. I could feel them. I felt like they were watching me. I kept hearing that gravelly voice say, "I was sent to kill you." With my head right up against the window. I turned my fan on, prayed for protection, and went to sleep.

I never heard anything that night. When I got up the next morning, Kirk was asleep on the couch next to the front door. He said that right after I went to bed, the wind picked up, the windows shook violently, and the front door knob rattled like someone was trying to get in. All night the wind howled. We went outside and saw downed tree limbs all around our little house, but not one single limb down anywhere else in town. I don't mean a little stick here or there, I'm talking about big limbs down. After we arrived at the church, we asked the Mennonites, who stayed in a tent just about a mile away, about their experience in the storm, but they hadn't heard anything that night.

That was my first day with a witch.

CHAPTER 2

DAY 2

DAY 2

I awoke the next morning, feeling excited about the previous evening's events at the tent meeting. I walked out of my room to see Kirk on the couch, awake, but looking very tired. Kirk, Angela and myself met at the table for some coffee. Kirk and Angela began to tell me of all the events I missed while I slept. The wind, the tree branches falling…the door handle rattling. Kirk was tired from sleeping on the couch. He said he had lost count of how many times he thought someone was coming in the front door. He prayed in tongues most of the night, as well as Angela.

In the morning service, Kirk ministered the Word. Angelique was struggling physically. Her alcohol and heroin addictions were coming to an end. Her body was not happy about her choices. Her body had been much abused through drug, alcohol and sexual abuse. She had prostituted herself out at times and later would share how she used sex as a power over people.

The team and I prayed for Angelique and visited with her further, and it seemed to relieve much of her physical and mental stress. She shared with us how she would drink a bottle of alcohol at night just to try and fall asleep. We came back that evening and once again, she was struggling and had been sick all day. She looked horrible. Her skin was white and pasty looking, kind of slimy looking, and her eyes looked very tired.

We ministered the healing anointing to her that night, and she seemed to experience a touch of what God had for her. She instantly could tell a difference in her health. This excited her. She was overflowing with questions that we tried to answer as we went. We were more concerned with getting her to focus on God's love for her, and how she was forgiven. The devil had been trying to make her feel guilty and condemned the whole way through. She was being pressured to give up. It was because she felt like there was just no way that God could possibly love her. We assured her it would all become progressively clearer in time. She continually told us, "You have no idea what I have done to people, and you have no idea what I was about to do to you. If you knew, you wouldn't love me, and God wouldn't love me."

I continued to show Angelique scripture examples of others whom God loved, in spite of the fact that they had failed him. For example, David committed adultery and then had a most loyal soldier murdered to cover up his deed.

The Apostle Paul was first known as Saul. Saul was responsible for families in the early church being violently torn apart from one another, imprisoned and many were martyred because of their faith in the Messiah, Jesus. After Saul had a vision of Jesus Christ, he was radically transformed. The former murderer became a New Creation in Christ and God used him to pen about two-thirds of the New Testament. We each shared parts of our personal testimonies, but really we didn't have much to offer in our own stories, seeing that she had been the High Witch of the Four Corners. We struggled a little to try and show her just how much God loved her.

The people of that town, including the very people who were in that tent with us, didn't like Angelique much. She had effected most of their lives negatively in one way or another. Twenty plus years serving Satan, and here we are on day two, trying to unravel all of this that has been put in her. Just a few days ago, we and God were her enemies. We had no idea that God was going to use a few supernatural signs to help her understand how much He really cared about her.

That night as we came back to the little cabin we were staying in, something was not right. As we pulled up to the cabin, we had left the light on by the door. There were also a couple of street lights surrounding the property. Yet, it seemed unusually dark that evening—noticeably dark—like the lights were not actually lighting up the areas around them. They were like pin holes, surrounded in darkness, and all of us mentioned the presence of evil that we sensed surrounding us.

Again, not trying to give into fear, we didn't want to talk about it too much, but everyone was noticeably a bit edgy and seemed to be more aware of our surroundings. I told Kirk and Angela that I was going to go outside to make a phone call to my wife because I felt like we were being intimidated by this evil presence, and I refused to give into that.

I placed my call and began walking down the road. It was so dark, really dark. As I walked, I could tell that I was not alone. It felt like the first time I met Angelique. Somewhere in that darkness, eyes were focused on me. So I determined to walk a bit further, even as the hair on my neck began to stand on end. So as not to startle my wife, I gave her all the great reports and talked a good talk, but I had an awareness that I was being stalked.

By the time I finished my phone call, I was about one-half mile away from the cabin and surrounded in complete darkness. Goose bumps were coming up on my arms, all my senses were on high alert. My hearing seemed to lock onto noises of all kinds. I glared at my surroundings as my vision adjusted to the darkness.

Suddenly the bushes rattled. I fully expected someone to jump out…but nothing. The wind began to whip around me, yet there was no breeze. I began to notice a sudden drop in the air temperature surrounding me as I walked. It was a thick, wet, cold air. There almost seemed to be a voice in it. I could feel fear tightening its grip on my throat. For a moment, I feared for my life. There was a real sense of urgency that something was about to happen. I've been in my share of fights before, and could normally be somewhat prepared for a physical encounter, but this seemed more real than any physical opponent that I had ever stood before. This opponent was invisible to the human eye…but real, none-the-less.

I noticed my walking took on a bit of a jog. My heart was pounding, my ears were ringing trying to listen for what was coming, and where it might be coming from. Suddenly, I stopped in my tracks. I began to grow angry at myself for almost giving in. One side note…never let your enemy see you sweat. I reminded myself that I am a man with authority.

Jesus said, "Behold, I give unto you power to tread on serpents and scorpions, and over all the power of the enemy: and nothing shall by any means hurt you."

—Luke 10:19 KJV

Then, I yelled, "Devil! You are not going to intimidate me! If someone is following me, then show yourself and let's do this right here, right now!" I was thinking that it could be some of Angelique's family. She had mentioned kidnappings before. I prepared myself to face them head on.

I'm glad no one was watching me; they may have thought I was nuts, yelling into the dark night at nothing, but it wasn't nothing. "Come on and show yourself you coward. Is that all you got? Wind tricks and rattling bushes? If you are gonna do something, then come on! I'm right here and I'm not going anywhere. Where are you? Chicken?" I started walking again. Now, I was getting mouthy with the devil.

"You aren't going to win this time. Your time is up here. I have been given all authority and power over all the power of the enemy, and nothing, nothing devil, can in any way harm me! You can't do it! I'm coming for you! I'm not going to run from you, I'm coming for you! There's a new sheriff in town, and he rules over all the powers, principalities, and dominions and every name that is or could ever be named and as sure as I feel you trying to walk with me, there is another who sticks closer than a brother. His name is JESUS! Remember Him, devil? He saw you fall from heaven like lightening. He's in me, and I'm telling you right now, if it's a fight you want, then a fight you shall have. Angelique is not yours anymore! You tried and you failed, and we are still here. If you are so bad, why are we still alive? You can't kill us and you know you can't!"

This encounter was so real to me that I fully expected Satan, himself, to walk out of those bushes on the side of the road. But nothing. When you truly know your authority, you will realize that you have more to intimidate the enemy with, than he has to intimidate you with. I made it back to the cabin and told them of all the conversations and events that just took place. We prayed together and went our separate ways to bed.

Once again, Kirk found himself struggling to sleep with the noises outside the cabin that night, all night. I slept just fine. Could it have been the spirit of God, or maybe the fan I ran on high to minimize the noise? Perhaps it was a combination of the two. Regardless, day two had come to a close.

CHAPTER 3

DAY 3

DAY 3

We all made it to the tent that morning to find a handful of people ready for a revival. TJ delivered the morning message. Noticeably absent was Angelique. It was a bit disturbing to us, but we prayed for her and believed that she would be alright. We tried to contact a few people to see if they knew of her location, but no one seemed to know where she was.

We went on with our day as normal. We ate lunch and talked with Pastor Ray and some of the town folk. We came back to the tent that evening and had a great time of healing. A few miracles even took place. But once again, no Angelique.

After the evening meeting, Kirk, Angela, TJ, Pastor Ray and I, along with a few of our fiends that traveled to support the meetings gathered outside the tent under a big tree back behind the church. We all discussed the amazing events of the past few meetings.

When asked, Pastor Ray indicated that he had no idea about Angelique's whereabouts. Pastor Ray was about to tell us more about Angelique's background when a van came flying into the parking lot right next to the tree we were gathered under. We were all a bit startled, still fully expecting some sort of an attack from her family. The van came in so fast, we thought someone was trying to run us over. It was the woman we sent Angelique home with on that first day. She jumped out of the van, very upset.

"I'm terribly sorry. Angelique insisted that I bring her back to you quickly. She received a phone call from her family, and she's all upset. I don't know what to do with her. She's going crazy."

Angelique stumbled out of the van like a drunk man might. She was sobbing so hard, we had to physically help her stand up. Someone went and got a chair for her. She was shaking so badly, we couldn't hardly understand a word she was saying. Finally she was able to articulate in a low, terrifying voice, "You're dead...you're dead..." We were all looking at each other when she lifted up her head, looked straight at me and said, "I'm so sorry, Donnie. I'm so sorry. You are a dead man!"

"What are you talking about? Why am I dead? What do you mean?"

We made her sit down. She could hardly stand up and was crying so hard.

"Donnie they know. They know what you did. You are a dead man. They are coming for you. They are going to kill you. Curses have been put in place already. I was supposed to kill but didn't. Now *they* are going to kill you Donnie!"

Angelique's every statement grew in volume and intensity.

"Who's coming?"

"The family is coming. My family is going to kill you. My mom called me and said, 'What have you done? What have you done? I know what you are doing Angelique!' The demons told her what happened. They reported back to her. She knows everything. She knows your name! She knew the second I got saved."

Her parents live in Joplin which is about forty-five minutes north of Chetopa. They are witches also. Her father and mother are witches, along with her sisters, brother, uncles, and some of her cousins. They run a gang called "The White Honkeys." They control the heroin trade from southwest Missouri, down through central Oklahoma—really bad guys. Later we discovered this was why Angelique had been placed over this area. She was the protector of the drug route...the High Witch of the Four Corners.

"You are a dead man. I'm so sorry Donnie. I'm so sorry."

Without thinking, without hesitating, these words rose up out of me. I said, "Where do they want to meet?"

She said, "What?"

I again said, "Where do they want to meet? I'll meet them anywhere at any time."

"Donnie, they will kill you. You don't understand who these people are and what you have done."

"You call them and ask them where they want to meet. I'll meet them. Anywhere. Anytime."

"Donnie you are a dead man. You will not make it out alive. You have no idea what you are dealing with here! They are powerful people. They will kill you and nobody will be able to save you. You will not make it out alive."

"Angelique, you were supposed to kill me right? Well here I am, and there you are. Tell them I will meet then anywhere at any time. They can name the place and the time."

I didn't do this out of arrogance. Somehow, inside, I felt like I was up against the prophets of Baal. (Please take time to read the account below.) I had no idea that I truly was. I remembered the end of that story in First Kings chapter eighteen* and felt mine would end the same. We prayed with her until she calmed down, and sent her back to rest at the woman's home where she had been staying. That evening, Angelique placed the phone call to her mother and told her what I had said.

*1 Kings 18:21-40 (NASB)

[21] Elijah came near to all the people and said, "How long will you hesitate between two opinions? If the LORD is God, follow Him; but if Baal, follow him." But the people did not answer him a word. [22] Then Elijah said to the people, "I alone am left a prophet of the LORD, but Baal's prophets are 450 men. [23] Now let them give us two oxen; and let them choose one ox for themselves and cut it up, and place it on the wood, but put no fire under it; and I will prepare the other ox and lay it on the wood, and I will not put a fire under it. [24] Then you call on the name of your god, and I will call on the name of the LORD, and the God who answers by

fire, He is God." And all the people said, "That is a good idea." ²⁵ So Elijah said to the prophets of Baal, "Choose one ox for yourselves and prepare it first for you are many, and call on the name of your god, but put no fire under it." ²⁶ Then they took the ox which was given them and they prepared it and called on the name of Baal from morning until noon saying, "O Baal, answer us." But there was no voice and no one answered. And they leaped about the altar which they made. ²⁷ It came about at noon, that Elijah mocked them and said, "Call out with a loud voice, for he is a god; either he is occupied or gone aside, or is on a journey, or perhaps he is asleep and needs to be awakened." ²⁸ So they cried with a loud voice and cut themselves according to their custom with swords and lances until the blood gushed out on them. ²⁹ When midday was past, they raved until the time of the offering of the evening sacrifice; but there was no voice, no one answered, and no one paid attention. ³⁰ Then Elijah said to all the people, "Come near to me." So all the people came near to him. And he repaired the altar of the LORD which had been torn down. ³¹ Elijah took twelve stones according to the number of the tribes of the sons of Jacob, to whom the word of the LORD had come, saying, "Israel shall be your name." ³² So with the stones he built an altar in the name of the LORD, and he made a trench around the altar, large enough to hold two measures of seed. ³³ Then he arranged the wood and cut the ox in pieces and laid it on the wood. ³⁴ And he said, "Fill four pitchers with water and pour it on the burnt offering and on the wood." And he said, "Do it a second time," and they did it a second time. And he said, "Do it a third time," and they did it a third time. ³⁵ The water flowed around the altar and he also filled the trench with water. ³⁶ At the time of the offering of the evening sacrifice, Elijah the prophet came near and said, "O LORD, the God of Abraham, Isaac and Israel, today let it be known that You are God in Israel and that I am Your servant and I have done all these things at Your word. ³⁷ Answer me, O LORD, answer me, that this people may know that You, O LORD, are God, and that You have turned their heart back again." ³⁸ Then the fire of the LORD fell and consumed the burnt offering and the wood and the stones and the dust, and licked up the water that was in the trench. ³⁹ When all the people saw it, they fell on their faces; and they said, "The LORD, He is God; the LORD, He is God." ⁴⁰ Then Elijah said to them, "Seize the *prophets of Baal; do not let one of them escape." So they seized them; and Elijah brought them down to the brook Kishon, and slew them there.*

When I arrived at the cabin that evening, Kirk and Angela were quick to express their concerns about the challenge I had made to Angelique's parents. Angela especially thought this was a very bad idea. Kirk kept silent knowing that I was going to go no matter what anyone else thought. We couldn't back down now. I had peace about what I had said. It was not a peace like everything was going to be easy. I knew in my spirit that it was in all likelihood going to be a nasty fight. But, I also was certain that if I would trust in my God, He would more than meet the challenge.

Angela was trying to be the voice of reason about the whole thing and hoped to get me to slow down and to really think this through. Angela "mothers" us on our trips. I say this with a heart of gratitude. At this point, I thought, some reassurance might help. I made some phone calls. I called a good friend of mine to discuss all that had taken place, and the challenge I had made.

"Don't do it! You need to be careful; these people are for real, and you need to really think about this. I don't recommend it..."

The conversation went on for a while about how I probably shouldn't do this. So I hung up and contacted my own mother. Certainly, she knows me and will tell me that I'm right! But no; she is *my mom*.

"Donnie, you need to really be careful here."

Next, I called my wife. I fully anticipated her to remind me that I have a family and how I need to stop being so forceful, trying to prove something. Just as I had all this figured out in my head as to what she was about to say, she said, "So when are you going?" My wife is an amazing person. She continued, "When you going? I'll be praying for you." Later, Kirk assured me that I would not be making that trip by myself, and that he would be there as well.

During this time, I felt God with me in a way that I had never experienced before. It was a calm assurance that what He said to me in His word, He would absolutely back up in my life in real time, in a real place called Chetopa, Kansas. As I walked back to the cabin thinking about what an amazing wife I have, I began to be saddened by the thought of how many believers do not exercise their God-given authority over the devil. That's all this was! Had they not read the Bible? Had they forgotten all the great stories of those who stood up to the devil, and though placed in harm's way, they were supernaturally protected? How about the three Hebrew boys? What about the account of Daniel and the lions' den? Sure, they were in great jeopardy, but they walked out! I was so disappointed and annoyed that I didn't find people who would just jump on board with me and say, "Go get 'em!"

When I returned from making phone calls, we met at the kitchen table. I told the team about the conversations that had just taken place. We prayed and then went to our bedrooms for the evening. My heart was heavy that night. Only a small remnant of individuals in the Body of Christ have even the vaguest notion of the authority they possess in Him. I slept pretty well in spite of that. I had no idea what was about to take place over the next few days. The devil was about to ramp it up on us, but God would not be outdone.

CHAPTER 4

DAY 4

DAY 4

The revival itself was going well. We witnessed blind eyes open, deaf ears hear, and many others healed of different types of pain and oppression. It was truly an authentic revival. Most of the people that were coming had no idea of the real fight that was taking place over their town. They could see the obvious—a woman who had troubled and upset their lives was now saved. But there was so much more going on in the spiritual realm.

This day started off like all the other days. After the morning meeting, we discussed having a big community outreach on the final day of the meeting. Kirk, Angela, TJ, Pastor Ray and I drove around Joplin looking for supplies for the event. That afternoon, we headed back to Chetopa. It was a beautiful day. The sun was shining and our spirits were high...not a cloud in the sky. From all appearances, it seemed we would, once again, have some tremendously pleasant weather for the evening service.

While in Joplin, we bought a Bible for Angelique. This would be her first Bible...first Christian Bible anyway; she owned a satanic one. Though inexpensive, it was the nicest Bible they had in stock. It really wasn't anything special...a fake leather, maroon-colored Bible. We decided that we would put some quick references in the front for her so she could turn to those scriptures when she needed encouragement.

We had just returned to the church and unloaded the supplies into the building, when suddenly, we heard something. "Is that the tornado siren going off?" Indeed, it was. We walked outside. Just moments earlier, it was sunny and clear. Almost right on top of us, was this huge, swirling, mass of dark green clouds, with a small funnel starting to form.

There was absolutely no shelter in the church, but Pastor informed us of a community shelter about one-half mile down the road. We all scrambled for the cars and took off towards the shelter. I had borrowed a friend's car. It was the most beautiful Dodge Challenger I had ever seen...top speed of 182 mph, bright yellow and amazing. I remember calling my wife while I was looking in the rearview mirror at the funnel cloud.

> "You won't believe where I am; I'm in the yellow jacket, looking at a tornado in my rearview mirror!"

> Her response was amusing. "Get off the phone and get that car somewhere safe!"

We arrived at the shelter only to find a few of the town's people gathered outside waiting on the person with the key. *No one had a key to the shelter.* There was some discussion of breaking in when, suddenly, a huge bolt of lightning hit a tree about twenty yards from us. Lightning continued to strike, with the environment filled with deafening thunder. Lightning was all around us. Suddenly, we looked up to see the funnel cloud right on top of us again; it seemed to be following us!

Someone mentioned the school shelter across town. We quickly got back into the vehicles. Everyone headed out and we made it to the school on the other side of town. We found most of the town and emergency personnel there. School had been in session. All of the students were indoors with hundreds of other people who came seeking shelter. At that moment, TJ got out of her car and said, "I've had enough! I'm not running anymore. She looked at me as if to say, "Well, aren't you coming?" So my Mennonite friend, Leon, and I walked to the side of the school. Sirens blaring....the tornado had reversed direction; it seemed to be following us. There it was again, all the way on the other side of town. We walked past all the emergency personnel. TJ walked right out into the open. Lightning was striking all around us. Leon was on her left; I stood to her right. TJ began to yell at that funnel cloud like it was a spoiled brat.

"How dare you try to harm us! Who do you think you are? You stop this right now in Jesus' name, and you dissipate in the name of Jesus! Devil, you have no authority here."

Leon and I remained fixed on the storm that was about to hit the school. Every time she would speak the name of Jesus, the funnel cloud would go back up into those swirling clouds, and would then try to come down again. She finally said with a commanding voice, "That's it; you dissipate in the name of Jesus!" Suddenly, the storm was gone. It wasn't a gradual departure; it was just gone. Over. Finished.

Over to my right, there was a woman smoking a cigarette, who witnessed the entire thing. She stood there staring at the sky in total amazement. She took one more slow puff off her cigarette, never turning her view from the sky. She slowly exhaled as she tossed her cigarette to the ground. Undoubtedly, this was a day she would never forget.

The emergency response team, located behind us, stood there silently. The air radios blared as someone on the other end requested a status report. One of the men at the school clicked his radio and replied,

"It's gone."

"What do you mean it's gone? How much damage do you have? How many injured?"

"None, it's gone, it's just gone."

"What's gone? Is the school gone?"

"There is no damage to report; it's just gone. The tornado, the storm…it's just gone."

People stood in silence watching TJ walk by. We went inside to find Kirk, doing what Kirk does. He and Angela were ministering to the people inside. We all returned to our cars and drove back to the church. TJ declined to ride. "I think I'll walk back, I need some time alone!" I watched as TJ walked right down the middle of the street with a little swagger that day.

Angelique later asked me, "How did you like that tornado? My parents sent that to kill you." A man that had been with Angelique during the tornado, later came privately to me and said,

"When the sirens went off, Angelique had just finished talking with her mom on the phone. He said, "When she heard the sirens, she ran to her room. I could hear her rummaging through something. She bolted out the front door to the front lawn. He told me that he ran behind her yelling, "What are you doing?" He ran outside and found her with a dagger of some sort in her hands. She was on her knees in the yard, with this dagger over her head, yelling something he could not understand. He ran over, grabbed her arm, and said,

"What are you doing?"

"I've got to stop this tornado!"

"No, this isn't how we do it. You don't work a spell against this. We have to *pray*."

Living in darkness was the only life Angelique had ever known up to this point. Though the new birth is immediate, one must be taught and their mind renewed in order to be able to walk in total freedom. He took the dagger from her, made her come inside and began to teach her how to pray.

That evening, before the service, we presented Angelique with her first Bible. I wish every person could see how this woman reacted to receiving this book. She began to tear up as she looked at us. She said, "This is *mine*? This is *my Bible*? She took the Bible and pressed it up against her chest like she had just received a newborn baby. She clinched it, held it tight and kept staring at it. She couldn't utter a word. Tears flowed as she held it tight against her chest over and over again, looking at it as if she just couldn't believe it.

We started the revival that evening with singing and testimonies. We heard reports from those who had been healed or helped in some way during the services. TJ shared, along with others, what we had witnessed take place that afternoon with the tornado. Angelique was sitting there listening. After I ministered that night, Angelique came forward with a bit of urgency. She looked very troubled. She began to ask about the Holy Spirit. I remember thinking, "What could she know about the Holy Spirit?" While our team prayed with others, I could hear TJ explaining to her about the Baptism of the Holy Spirit. Eventually the entire team joined the conversation. Angelique spoke with urgency and seemed very troubled. "I've got to have the Holy Spirit. I've got to speak in tongues." What did she know about speaking in tongues? This girl was about to work a spell on a storm about 4 hours earlier. Now she is standing there enquiring about the Holy Spirit and speaking in tongues. "I've got to have it, I need it." So we explained how to receive, and then we prayed. Not even a minute later, she was baptized in the Holy Spirit and she was speaking in tongues fluently.

God has not left the believer without resources. The following scriptures talk about supernatural weaponry.

2 Corinthians 10:3-4 KJV

³ For though we walk in the flesh, we do not war after the flesh: ⁴ For the weapons of our warfare are not carnal, but mighty through God to the pulling down of strong holds;

Ephesians 6:10-18 ESV

The Whole Armor of God

¹⁰ Finally, be strong in the Lord and in the strength of his might. ¹¹ Put on the whole armor of God, that you may be able to stand against the schemes of the devil. ¹² For we do not wrestle against flesh and blood, but against the rulers, against the authorities, against the cosmic powers over this present darkness, against the spiritual forces of evil in the heavenly places. ¹³ Therefore take up the whole armor of God, that you may be able to withstand in the evil day, and having done all, to stand firm. ¹⁴ Stand therefore, having fastened on the belt of truth, and having put on the breastplate of righteousness, ¹⁵ and, as shoes for your feet, having put on the readiness given by the gospel of peace. ¹⁶ In all circumstances take up the shield of faith, with which you can extinguish all the flaming darts of the evil one; ¹⁷ and take the helmet of salvation, and the sword of the Spirit, which is the word of God, *¹⁸ praying at all times in the Spirit, with all prayer and supplication. To that end, keep alert with all perseverance, making supplication for all the saints…*

Empowered

The gift of the Holy Spirit baptism first occurred on the Day of Pentecost. This gift has been available ever since. The only prerequisite is that you must first trust in Jesus alone for your salvation, confessing Him as Lord.

The Holy Spirit will move on your vocal cords, lips and tongues, but it's up to you to put the sound into action and speak forth boldly in faith. The Spirit gives the utterance, but it's up to us to receive by faith and do the speaking.

Acts 2:4 KJV

⁴ And they were all filled with the Holy Ghost, and began to speak with other tongues, as the Spirit gave them utterance.

Notice again, *they* were filled and spoke…the Spirit gave them utterance.

Acts 1:4-5, 8 NLT

"Do not leave Jerusalem until the Father sends you the gift he promised, as I told you before. ⁵ John baptized with[a] water, but in just a few days you will be baptized with the Holy Spirit.

*⁸ But you will receive **power** when the Holy Spirit comes upon you. And you will be my witnesses, telling people about me everywhere—in Jerusalem, throughout Judea, in Samaria, and to the ends of the earth."*

In verse 8, the Greek word "dunamis" is translated "power" which means "miracle working ability". The Baptism in the Holy

Spirit was not intended to be an optional experience. New Testament Christianity was to include authority and power. This was the subject of Jesus' last recorded sermon. After Jesus' resurrection, He was seen by over five-hundred people, but only one-hundred twenty of them chose to obey Him. His mother Mary was one. His instructions were simple: wait until power comes. Like all things in the Kingdom of God, the Baptism in the Holy Spirit must be received by faith.

The Baptism in the Holy Spirit was God's idea, so it is not necessary to beg or convince Him to empower us. Nor do we need to fear anything false. When a born-again child of God asks the Heavenly Father for this blessed empowerment, God will not give Him a substitute.

Luke 11:11-13 KJV

11 If a son shall ask bread of any of you that is a father, will he give him a stone? or if he ask a fish, will he for a fish give him a serpent? 12 Or if he shall ask an egg, will he offer him a scorpion? 13 If ye then, being evil, know how to give good gifts unto your children: how much more shall your heavenly Father give the Holy Spirit to them that ask him?

Anointed for Service

Jesus, of course is our example in all things. Jesus, Himself, was anointed and empowered by the Holy Spirit.

Acts 10:38 NLT

38 And you know that God anointed Jesus of Nazareth with the Holy Spirit and with power. Then Jesus went around doing good and healing all who were oppressed by the devil, for God was with him.

Mark 16:15-17 ESV

15 And he said to them, "Go into all the world and proclaim the gospel to the whole creation." 16 Whoever believes and is baptized

will be saved, but whoever does not believe will be condemned.
*¹⁷ And these signs will accompany those who believe: in my name they will cast out demons; they will speak in new **tongues**;*

In plain English, the above verse indicates that speaking in tongues would be one of the signs which would accompany future converts of Christianity.

Acts 2:3-4 KJV

*And there appeared unto them cloven **tongues** like as of fire, and it sat upon each of them. And they were all filled with the Holy Ghost, and began to speak with other **tongues**, as the Spirit gave them utterance.*

Since the Spirit is giving the utterance, we know that we are praying the perfect will of God, for the Holy Spirit would not inspire any other kind of prayer except that which is accordance with the perfect will of the Trinity.

Acts 2:11 KJV
*Cretes and Arabians, we do hear them speak in our **tongues** the wonderful works of God.*

Acts 10:46 KJV
*For they heard them speak with **tongues**, and magnify God.*

The glossolalia phenomenon (speaking in tongues) is both a tool in worship, declaring the wonderful works of God and a means of recharging your spiritual battery.

Jude 20 KJV
But ye, beloved, building up yourself on your most holy faith, praying in the Holy Ghost.

In the following passage, note that the Spirit's empowerment was not limited to first generation Christians, but it belongs to you too.

Acts 2:39

For the promise is for you and for your children and for all who are far off, everyone whom the Lord our God calls to himself.

The promise referred to here is the promise that Jesus made of the Baptism in the Holy Spirit.

Though in the initial account of Acts chapter 2, no one had hands laid upon them, it is clear from the following scripture that Paul had a ministry along that lines.

Acts 19:6 KJV
And when Paul had laid his hands upon them, the Holy Ghost came on them; and they spake with tongues, and prophesied.

Paul had freely received, and was empowered to freely give. He was a practitioner of praying and speaking in the Spirit.

1 Corinthians 14:18 KJV
*I thank my God, I speak with **tongues** more than ye all:*

Angelique later explained to us that they (witches), know all too well the power of the Holy Spirit and tongues. She explained that when Christians speak in tongues, there are always supernatural results—cause and effect—just as their spells produced results. She said that when Christians speak in tongues, that they (witches) do not know what to do with that. They don't understand how to combat that. She said, "We know all the languages of the world, but we just can't figure that one out, and so we don't know how to come against someone who is baptized in the Holy Spirit, who speaks in tongues." She said, "That's why I have to have it. It's the only safe way to combat the evil forces."

When Angelique began to speak in tongues, she stopped and a big grin came over her face. She said, "What was that? I've never felt power like this before." You couldn't get that big old smile off her face. We wanted to make sure she understood this was something that she now possessed and that she didn't need to be with us in order to pray in tongues. We explained that praying in tongues is not a one-time thing. So we instructed her to speak in tongues at will, to stop at will and then to begin again, not based on emotion, rather faith. We helped her understand that this experience was not a spell or incantation; this was the mighty Holy Spirit moving in and through her. She told us that she knew this to be so...that this presence and power was unlike anything she had ever experienced.

Everyone was excited and talking about all the day's events. People lingered after service that night, not wanting to leave the environment of peace that had come. All of a sudden, someone ran into the tent. "Did you feel that?" It was a 3.2 magnitude earthquake as we later found out from the US Geological Survey. Angelique looked at me with big eyes and said, "The devil is losing his grip!"

A witch, a tornado, and an earthquake—amazing!

After the evening service, we headed back to our little cabin again. I called my wife and told her of all the things that had taken place. It seemed she was more concerned about the car than my life. (Not really, but it was funny to hear her talk about the car She wanted to make sure that it was ok. After all, it was borrowed and worth more than our house.) We gathered around the table and talked about the testimonies that had been given and all the events of the day. We were pretty wound up. We all finally went to bed. I missed the next few hours. I turned on the fan, talked with God, and out I went.

When I awoke the next morning, I found Kirk sitting on the couch, looking sleepy like he hadn't slept. "What happened? Did I miss something?" He and Angela explained to me that during the night, around 3:30 a.m., one of the most severe thunderstorms they had ever experienced rolled through the area. They shared how they thought maybe another tornado was being sent to try and catch us off guard while we slept. They told me that the lightening was the worst they had ever seen. As TJ had done earlier, Kirk commanded the storm to dissipate. He said that within 30 seconds after using the name of Jesus, the storm ended suddenly.

CHAPTER 5

DAY 5

DAY 5

The next morning, we walked outside and once again saw tree limbs lying all over the place, and leaves scattered everywhere. It looked like a big storm had come through the previous evening just as Angela and Kirk had reported. We went to the church for the morning meeting, about 1 mile away from our cabin. Kirk asked our Mennonite friends about the previous evening storm. They were camping in a tent next to the revival tent, and we assumed that they would certainly have heard the big storm that blew through. Nothing. No storm, no tree limbs—they heard absolutely nothing—1 mile away! Kirk asked Pastor Ray who lived right next to the church, "Did you hear anything?" Nothing!

Later, when we were talking with Angelique, she asked us if we had experienced a storm. She said that once again, her family was trying to scare us away. I asked her about the meeting with her parents. "Are we going to meet? I'm ready. When and where?" Angelique told me that after the evening storm, her mother called her and told her that they were not going to meet with me.

Angelique also told us that her brother had contacted her privately and wanted to meet with us because he realized that Angelique was now more powerful than ever, and he wanted out. He wanted what she had. He wanted to meet us in another county in an area where his family didn't have authority. Angelique explained it to us using the analogy of cell service. She said that there were some places where they couldn't *see* and *hear* (supernaturally) what was going on. Angelique's brother wanted to meet with us, but he was very afraid and wasn't sure that he could do so without being found out by his family. So many broken individuals turn to the dark arts. We were created to have a relationship with a supernatural God. This is what we crave, but too often people resort to the dark side to fill that inner void. The power to manipulate and control situations and people entices so many, but they continue to grope for real peace in the dark void of a realm that is chaotic, fear-based and fear-driven.

The Authority of the Believer

The authority of the believer has been little taught in mainstream churches and even less understood. The number of scriptures which support the practice of using commands of faith, and the keys of binding and loosing are many. Here are a few.

Matthew 16:19 ESV

"I will give you the keys of the kingdom of heaven, and whatever you bind on earth shall be bound in heaven, and whatever you loose on earth shall be loosed in heaven."

You have heaven's backing. You are empowered to bind the enemy and loose blessing, healing, finances, and angelic intervention. Whatever Heaven has, is now yours. Whatever you have, now belongs to Him.

James 4:7 ESV

Submit yourselves therefore to God. Resist the devil, and he will flee from you.

You have what it takes to put the enemy on the run.

Luke 10:19-21 ESV

Behold, I have given you authority to tread on serpents and scorpions, and over all the power of the enemy, and nothing shall hurt you. Nevertheless, do not rejoice in this, that the spirits are subject to you, but rejoice that your names are written in heaven." In that same hour he rejoiced in the Holy Spirit and said, "I thank you, Father, Lord of heaven and earth, that you have hidden these things from the wise and understanding and revealed them to little children; yes, Father, for such was your gracious will.

Mark 16:17-20 ESV

And these signs will accompany those who believe: in my name they will cast out demons; they will speak in new tongues; they will pick up serpents with their hands; and if they drink any deadly poison, it will not hurt them; they will lay their hands on the sick, and they will recover." So then the Lord Jesus, after he had spoken to them, was taken up into heaven and sat down at the right hand of God. And they went out and preached everywhere, while the Lord worked with them and confirmed the message by accompanying signs.

1 Peter 5:8 ESV

Be sober-minded; be watchful. Your adversary the devil prowls around like a roaring lion, seeking someone to devour.

1 John 4:4 ESV

Little children, you are from God and have overcome them, for he who is in you is greater than he who is in the world.

Revelation 12:11 ESV

And they have conquered him by the blood of the Lamb and by the word of their testimony, for they loved not their lives even unto death.

John 14:12 ESV

Truly, truly, I say to you, whoever believes in me will also do the works that I do; and greater works than these will he do, because I am going to the Father.

Mark 11:23 ESV

Truly, I say to you, whoever says to this mountain, 'Be taken up and thrown into the sea,' and does not doubt in his heart, but believes that what he says will come to pass, it will be done for him.

Mark 6:13 ESV

And they cast out many demons and anointed with oil many who were sick and healed them.

Ephesians 1:20-22 ESV

That he worked in Christ when he raised him from the dead and seated him at his right hand in the heavenly places, far above all rule and authority and power and dominion, and above every name that is named, not only in this age but also in the one to come. And he put all things under his feet and gave him as head over all things to the church...

Matthew 28:18-20 ESV

And Jesus came and said to them, "All authority in heaven and on earth has been given to me. Go therefore and make disciples of all nations, baptizing them in the name of the Father and of the Son and of the Holy Spirit, teaching them to observe all that I have commanded you. And behold, I am with you always, to the end of the age."

Matthew 10:1 ESV

And he called to him his twelve disciples and gave them authority over unclean spirits, to cast them out, and to heal every disease and every affliction.

Psalm 91:13 ESV

You will tread on the lion and the adder; the young lion and the serpent you will trample underfoot.

Romans 16:20 ESV

The God of peace will soon crush Satan under your feet. The grace of our Lord Jesus Christ be with you.

Colossians 1:13 ESV

He has delivered us from the domain of darkness and transferred us to the kingdom of his beloved Son

Acts 16:18 ESV

And this she kept doing for many days. Paul, having become greatly annoyed, turned and said to the spirit, "I command you in the name of Jesus Christ to come out of her." And it came out that very hour.

Acts 3:6 ESV

But Peter said, "I have no silver and gold, but what I do have I give to you. In the name of Jesus Christ of Nazareth, rise up and walk!"

Luke 10:17-20 ESV

The seventy-two returned with joy, saying, "Lord, even the demons are subject to us in your name!" And he said to them, "I saw Satan fall like lightning from heaven. Behold, I have given you authority to tread on serpents and scorpions, and over all the power of the enemy, and nothing shall hurt you. Nevertheless, do not rejoice in this, that the spirits are subject to you, but rejoice that your names are written in heaven."

John 5:8 ESV

Jesus said to him, "Get up, take up your bed, and walk."

Revelation 12:10 ESV

And I heard a loud voice in heaven, saying, "Now the salvation and the power and the kingdom of our God and the authority of his Christ have come, for the accuser of our brothers has been thrown down, who accuses them day and night before our God.

Though Jesus was inherently God, he chose to walk as a man to purchase back the authority that King Adam had lost when he betrayed Him through disobedience. At the point of his disobedience, Adam forfeited mankind's authority. Consequently, there was a power shift in the earth. Since the first man caused mankind to fall from his position of authority, a man was required to put things back in order through obedience. This is why Jesus, of necessity, operated as a man under the enabling power of the Holy Spirit. We are anointed by this very same Holy Spirit.

Acts 10:38 KJV

38 How God anointed Jesus of Nazareth with the Holy Ghost and with power: who went about doing good, and healing all that were oppressed of the devil; for God was with him.

Made Right

One key to understanding that authority in the Name of Jesus belongs to people like you and me is to understand that we have been made right with God through the blood of Jesus. Notice these scriptures relating to *righteousness*.

Romans 5:17, 19 KJV

*17 For if by one man's offence death reigned by one; much more they which receive abundance of grace and of the **gift of righteousness** shall reign in life by one, Jesus Christ.) 19 For as by one man's disobedience many were made sinners, so by the obedience of one shall many be made **righteous**.*

Righteousness simply means "right standing" with God. Notice that we have been given righteousness as a GIFT through Jesus. It is through this gift that we dominate our turf.

2 Corinthians 5:17 KJV

17 Therefore if any man be in Christ, he is a new creature: old things are passed away; behold, all things are become new.

The eternal part of us becomes brand new with the nature of Jesus when we invite Him to become our Lord and Savior. Knowing who you are in Christ is vital to working in your authority.

2 Corinthians 5:21 KJV

[21] For he hath made him to be sin for us, who knew no sin; that we might be made the righteousness of God in him.

It was through divine exchange that we were made righteous with His righteousness. He became our sin on the cross. He paid the price. He became what we were, so that we could be like He is now.

This right standing with God is the basis for our authority. We have been made holy and clean. Our new identity through our union with Christ, qualifies us for both the empowerment of the Spirit, as well as the authority to use the name of Jesus as God's ambassadors.

2 Corinthians 5:20 ESV

[20] Therefore, we are ambassadors for Christ, God making his appeal through us. We implore you on behalf of Christ, be reconciled to God.

Now, the Father is inviting his children to work together with Him in the earth.

2 Corinthians 6:1 KJV

*We then, **as workers together with Him**, beseech you also that ye receive not the grace of God in vain.*

God's grace means that we have extraordinary favor with God and that nothing shall be impossible to us if we believe.

CHAPTER 6

DAY 6

DAY 6

On the sixth evening of our meeting, Angela asked the host Pastor if he had any heavy logging chains. He affirmed that he did and went to get them. As a teaching illustration, Angela took two heavy chains and wrapped Angelique up in the chains. Angela looked at Angelique and said, "It's time to break off those chains of bondage that have been holding you for so long." It was this simple, but powerful example that helped Angelique to experience a new level of freedom. We talked to her about how easy it really is to be free. It wasn't impossible. It was just as simple as her choosing to remove physical chains. We talked about our part to play in remaining free and how she needed to be a doer of the Word and not a hearer only.

After we instructed her, she made the observation that there is a parallel between how things work in the kingdom of light and the kingdom of darkness. She further explained that using chains to help someone understand that freedom belongs to them, was exactly how she was taught to work spells. She told me that in witchcraft, you have to physically work spells. You could read spells, but that wasn't enough. She explained that spells require speaking combined with some action in the natural, to possess the spiritual ability to work the spell in order to manipulate people and matter.

During this very same conversation, I asked her about the curses that she had placed on the town. I wanted to know how that worked, and exactly what she had done. I felt that it was time for her to remove those curses. I told her the Lord had led me to have a "reverse the curse tour." She was very anxious and fearful about doing that. She admitted multiple times that she was afraid to go back to those places and try to talk to those demons again. Nevertheless, she agreed to meet me the next morning.

CHAPTER 7

DAY 7

DAY 7

The seventh evening service would conclude the revival meetings. Kirk and I met with Angelique that morning to "reverse the curse" as planned. She said that in order to do this, we had three strategic places to go. Our first stop was at the entrance of the town.

We drove across the Neosho River off Highway 166. At the river bank, next to the park, we walked to a concrete boat ramp where she had placed the first curse. As you look across the river, you can see down the main street of the town. I asked Angelique what she had done there. She explained about a specific curse that she had uttered that night and how she released demons over the town. When I asked her what demons, she hesitated.

"Do I have to say their names?"

"Yes, tell me who."

"The main demons that I controlled..." (She paused staring at the river.) "I never did control them; they had full control over me. I was used and dedicated as a porthole for the demonic, meaning that whenever the higher witches wanted to release the demonic somewhere, they could use my body as a portal to do it. I had surrendered all my rights to my entire person. No matter where I was, or what was going on, if they wanted to summon the demonic, I would submit to that power and allow them to use me to do their will."

The devil has no authority. He has to attach to a human in order to use their authority. To have authority on the earth, you have to live in a body. This is why Jesus had to be born of a woman. The womb of a woman is the legal entry into this world. This is why demonic entities will seek to enter a person's body and/or their soul. The human body is the "earth suit" that has been provided for your journey through life on earth.

I asked her once again, "What are their names?"

"Baal…"

"Wait a minute! What did you say?"

"Baal."

"Do you have any idea who that is? Do you know he is talked about in the Bible?"

She had no idea. Kirk and I exchanged looks in utter amazement. We explained to her that Baal, and Asheroth, a Phoenician goddess, also known as Asherah, were both mentioned in the Bible.

Judges 3:7 NKJV
So the children of Israel did evil in the sight of the LORD. They forgot the LORD their God, and served the Baals and Asherahs.

2 Chronicles 33:3 NKJV
For he rebuilt the high places which Hezekiah his father had broken down; he raised up altars for the Baals, and made wooden images; and he worshiped all the host of heaven[a] and served them.

Judges 10:6 NKJV
Then the children of Israel again did evil in the sight of the LORD, and served the Baals and the Ashtoreths, the gods of Syria, the gods of Sidon, the gods of Moab, the gods of the people of Ammon, and the gods of the Philistines; and they forsook the LORD and did not serve Him.

She told us that Balaam was her most summoned god. Balaam…the Sun god. She said that all "the gods" were all tied together. Among other things, Balaam controlled weather patterns. She had no idea that these fallen entities were mentioned in the Bible. They were simply a real part of her daily life. Angelique also mentioned monuments that had been built to these gods.

After we had talked about these things, I told her that she was going to call every one of them by name, because they knew her voice. I told her that she was going to tell them to leave this area, that they were no longer authorized to rule as princes of the power of the air, and that they must go. I instructed her to denounce them in the name of Jesus Christ, and tell them that she now serves Jesus and no other.

She did not want to mention their names. She said, "You don't talk to them like that!" I said, "Oh yes, you do! Greater is he that is in you, Angelique. It's time to prove it." As she began, she said, "Baal..." suddenly her eyes turned black, and she tilted her head sideways. She let out a deep growl, and then she stopped and said, "Whoa...sorry...sorry; No! You do not have any power over me anymore." Angelique had learned how to yield to those demonic entities. Practice had made her perfect. The art of yielding was a natural as breathing to her. Imagine what could happen if Christians could become perfected in yielding to the Holy Spirit. We would have a perfect expression of the resurrected Christ in the earth today. Angelique stood on the exact spot that she cursed that town and released every curse and renounced every false god. She told them that they had no power there anymore, and that she would not be the carrier for them anymore. And then, she spoke a blessing over the town in place of the curse.

When we had finished there, she shared with us that though she was the one who pronounced the curse, it was actually the town that kept it activated. She told us how individuals in the community now curse the town out of their own mouths, and that even the pastors did so. She explained the importance of this location, because it was the entrance to the city line. She told us that it was important to start at the line so that everyone that drove over that line would be in her power. It's a sad commentary that too often those in darkness understand spiritual realities more than those who have been sitting in church pews for decades.

The spiritual principle of speaking a desired end was a common practice for Angelique. The following scriptures give us some further insight into what was going on here.

Luke 4:2, 5-8 KJV

Being forty days tempted of the devil. And in those days he [Jesus] did eat nothing: and when they were ended, he afterward hungered. [5] And the devil, taking him up into an high mountain, shewed unto him all the kingdoms of the world in a moment of time. [6] And the devil said unto him, All this power will I give thee, and the glory of them: for that is delivered unto me; and to whomsoever I will I give it. [7] If thou therefore wilt worship me, all shall be thine.

Notice that the enemy took Jesus to a high point from which, He was shown **all the kingdoms of the world in a moment of time.** This was a supernatural experience in which Jesus was shown everything that Satan had received when Adam forfeited his authority and dominion. This took place when Adam disobeyed God, committing high treason against Him. Satan said, **"All this power will I give thee, and the glory of them: for that is delivered unto me; and to whomsoever I will I give it."**

Who delivered the kingdoms of the world to Satan? Adam did when he sinned. God gave authority to Adam. Adam gave it to Satan. I would like to point out that Jesus experienced a legitimate temptation. In this particular case, if Satan had lied about what he had to offer, Jesus would have discerned that and no temptation would have taken place. I mention this story to simply point out that the enemy has stolen what belonged to man. Servants of the fallen one have learned how to tap into that authority even in their unregenerate state.

Since Jesus went to the cross as our sin substitute, and arose on the third day, the Church has had her authority restored. But since members of the Church on earth are either ignorant of their authority or simply choose not to exert the effort to use what they have been given, agents of the enemy illegitimately misuse human authority for selfish and satanic purposes. God has done His part; the ball is now in our court.

After Angelique had blessed the first location, we took a gravel road at the other end of town. We turned onto Wallace Road which connects Kansas and Oklahoma. This was the main backroad used to move drugs through. She took us to the exact place where she had worked this curse, and she reversed it just as she had the previous place.

After that second location, she opened up to us even more. She shared how she and her sister were used in child pornography and how dangerous and demonic porn is. She said, "If someone is looking at porn, you better know that we are looking at it with you!" She was speaking of their ability to *see* and *hear* through demonic empowerment.

Angelique went on to tell us that all these movies and cartoons about the spirit realm are all based on, in her words, "some real shit". Then she said, "Excuse my language, but when you see a cartoon that has someone using a spell in it, where do you think they came up with those words? Do you think they just made them up? Well, they didn't. They are real spells, and they are using them in cartoons to get to your kids. Do you think these movies about paranormal activity are fake? Donnie, these are real. That stuff is real, and it's the devil. I've watched them, and they are real; it's exactly what we do in our spells, and it's exactly what the demons do through us. All the cute witch and vampire movies—all these supernatural shows—are all based on reality of what we do. The entertainment industry is using real spells, working with real demons, and it's all done in such a way so as to allow things into you that you wouldn't normally allow."

Did you know that leaders in the New Age movement speak of a planned influence beginning in the educational branch, and then moving into the political and medical arenas? Dick Sutphen, New Ager and promoter of these changes, stated something to the effect that their goal as New Agers is to obscure terminology. In other words, once the occult, metaphysical and new age terminology is removed, he believes that New Agers will have concepts and techniques that will be very acceptable to the general public and hence, will open the New Age door to millions who normally would not be receptive. They are just changing the terminology, and the greater community is just eating it up— hook, line and sinker.

Our third destination was towards Oswego. We went to the other side of that town and ended up at a bend in the Neosho River off of Xavier Street. Angelique told us that she had cursed the town at this exact location. On this day, she renounced the curses and spoke a blessing over this area too.

At this third location, she told Kirk and me that when she had finished cursing that place, she made a cut on her hand, allowing the blood to run into the water of the Neosho River. She used the water of that river as a type of delivery system to carry her curse. "From this spot," she said, "let this water swallow up all who enter it." This location had a small underwater dam that helped to control the flow of the river. She told us that just two weeks after she had proclaimed that curse, a friend of hers saw two boys drowning who had slipped off this small dam. When her friend jumped in to save the boys, he himself drowned in that exact spot with them. She started to cry and ask for forgiveness as she removed that curse on the waterway. Instead of a curse, she now spoke blessing to go where ever the river would flow.

On our return trip home, Angelique told us that many in the local police force were also involved to one degree or another in the demonic. She said that they assisted her family's network of drug trafficking by turning a blind eye to what was going on. She said they did this mostly out of fear.

After we arrived back at the sight of our tent meetings, we began preparing for the evening service and the upcoming community outreach. We had bounce houses, free food and drinks. Angelique arrived with her four children. She wasn't supposed to have access to them. Her parents had been awarded legal custody of the children after Angelique attempted suicide after the Joplin tornado. This was especially surprising now that her family perceived her decision for Christ as personal betrayal. But somehow, miraculously, she was able to have them for that evening. (We later discovered this was part of a diabolical plan to try and destroy what we were doing.) She had two boys, age 13 and 10, and two daughters, 8 and 4.

As the rest of the team was working the last moments of the community outreach, I went back to shower and prepare to preach that night. Pastor Ray had told me that he expected us to have a packed out house that night. He had heard from many who were planning to attend.

This is Kirk's account of these events:

Kirk's Account:

After the community event, I was cleaning up the grounds. Angelique was outside smoking a cigarette when she started hollering at me, "Kirk! Kirk! Look up there!" As she pointed to the sky, I looked up to see a cross in the sky made from airplane exhaust. Seeing that I wasn't getting it, Angelique excitedly pointed out that it was over one of the places where we had reversed the curse earlier that day. I didn't think much of it at that time, but I could tell it meant everything to her. I continued cleaning, but she started yelling at me again. I looked up to see her pointing in an entirely different direction. Another cross appeared in the sky, but this time, it appeared to be over the end of town, across the river where we started out the day reversing the curse, While I was still looking at the second cross, she began to yell at me again, "Look, look!" I was startled to see a third cross in the sky. There was no doubt that this was over the third area that she had led us to, where we witnessed Angelique reverse the curse. At this point, I could not deny that God was giving her a moment of revelation of how real He is.

Kirk called me and asked me to step outside of the house, to look up and tell him what I saw. Sure enough, three undeniable crosses, all seeming to hover over the three places where Angelique had reversed the curse that day. Amazing.

The night when Angelique tried to take her life by slitting her own throat, her four children were with her. She did this in front of all these children. They had sat and watched their mother take a knife, run it across her throat and fall over, bleeding, right in front of them.

Angelique spoke of the fear she had of her thirteen-year-old son who was just starting to be controlled by demonic activity. She told us how a supernatural strength would overtake him. He would become violent, black out and not remember anything he had done. He had already had some run-ins with the police at thirteen. She told me that one night she awoke to him sitting on her chest strangling her. She wrestled him to the floor to free herself from his grip.

This thirteen year old boy told us that periodically he would see a red-horned demon, and how when he saw that demon, he wouldn't remember anything after that until he would wake up somewhere else feeling exhausted.

The ten year old son had been living in fear. He would see things that others couldn't see…dark things.

The 8 year old daughter would only sleep with the light on and was constantly afraid to go to sleep at night because of the man who would come in the dark.

The 4 year old daughter would have visions of vampires. Later that evening, during the service, she was discovered drawing satanic symbols in crayon on paper, not just scary faces, but actual ritualistic, satanic symbols.

We began the service. Angelique and her 4 children sat on the front row. We were meeting indoors for this last meeting due to the falling, cool temperatures in the October air. The place was packed out. From where I was standing in front, we had the well-dressed, mostly over-sixty-church crowd. On the other side was Angelique, her children, and some of the locals, members of the church, as well as some visitors. The service started off as normal. Suddenly, a woman about half way back on the right side, went into a seizure. We stopped and TJ, Kirk, Angela and a few others came and ministered to her. It was quite a distraction. I was suddenly beginning to pick up on what might be taking place. I was intrigued by the fact that these children were suddenly allowed to be with their mother who had turned her back on the family and the occult. Why would Angelique's parents allow her to take these children to a church service? Didn't they see what happened to Angelique?

It was starting to become clear. This was a well thought out plan. The woman who had the seizure recovered very quickly as they prayed over her. The whole time I was watching the people in the crowd. Observing Angelique and her children, I was trying to spiritually discern what was actually going on. I wasn't sure why I was unsettled, but was trying to piece it all together. I could see in the eyes of Pastor Ray's wife that she was very unsettled and even angry.

I tried to recover the service as best as possible after the woman's demonic seizure. The Lord impressed me to simply continue ministering. Just moments later, Kirk jumped up urgently as Angelique was motioning for him. As Kirk reached Angelique, her youngest son slumped over like a dead man. I thought, "The service is shot!" People were noticeably uncomfortable. They looked worried. Kirk, Angela, TJ and other visiting friends of ours were ministering to Angelique's son. Things were spinning out of control fast. The boy had passed out, unconscious. While they ministered to the younger boy, the oldest son became stiff as a board, sat straight up with eyes rolled back, and fell off of the pew onto the floor. He began rolling and mumbling something unintelligible.

Angelique was now holding the piece of paper that the 4 year old daughter had drawn of the satanic symbols. The oldest daughter had pulled her knees to her chest and buried her head into her knees, rocking back and forth. Angelique was in full panic mode.

As all this was taking place, Kirk was ministering to the youngest boy. Kirk was praying in the spirit in the boy's face. As he continued to pray, the boy finally opened his eyes; they were glassy, dark circles. Kirk asked him if he had seen the red-horned demon. He acknowledged that he had. Kirk asked him, "Would you like him to leave you alone?" They boy said, "Yes." Kirk cast that thing out of the boy, as it twisted and turned his body, torturing the boy as it left. When the demon had gone out of the boy, he sat there, a little bewildered. Kirk then asked him, "Would you want Jesus to help you from now on?" The boy answered in the affirmative and accepted Jesus as his Lord and Savior.

While that was taking place, someone came and sat by the girls and began to minister to them. The oldest son was on the floor surrounded by a group of praying believers. It was about this time that I made eye contact with the pastor's wife. She looked at me with tears in her eyes and disgust on her face. She then shot up and took off running out the back door. I jumped up and ran right after her. I found her outside between the church and the tent. I yelled, "Where do you think you are going?"

This woman got right up in my face and said, "I'm so mad. We finally got rid of her and finally were able to get the church built back up, and you let her back in here. I don't want her here! I don't want that in my church. She's already run everyone off and now you've brought her back in here. I want her gone!"

I looked that woman right in the eyes and said, "You get your butt back in there right now! How dare you run out of that church in a time like this! You get back in there right now. Go love the hell out of that woman right now!"

"I can't, I can't do it!"

I hugged her and said, "Yes you can. Yes you can, and yes you will. This is your church. You get in there and help your husband. You are empowered to help him. You get in there and go find Angelique. Give her a big hug and you love on her; let's go!"

(Though I spoke very directly to her, my relationship with these dear pastors warranted the words I spoke. They both know how very much I love them. When you are in the army of the Lord, and you are engaged in active combat, you better know whose instructions to obey and whom you can trust.)

We walked back in and she obeyed the command to love. By this time, things had settled down a bit, and I was able to talk to everyone else about what had just taken place. What was meant as an attack to disrupt, had backfired. All four children accepted Jesus as Lord that night.

After the service ended, the kids were just having fun and running around. It was the first time that evening that we saw them acting like care-free children. As we were visiting with Angelique and others, she called the kids over and asked them how they felt. They were just so happy. The youngest boy said, "Momma, will the red man come back again?" She said, "Nope, he will never come back baby." He smiled real big and took off running and you could hear him telling his siblings, "He won't be coming back tonight. And he told his little sister, "You can go to sleep tonight. He won't bother you anymore." The oldest son came over to us and asked, "Is it true? The man won't come in the dark anymore?" "Yep, that's right!" He was so excited. Unfortunately, we all knew these children would be returning to their grandparent's home soon. Little did we know, this was just the beginning of Angelique's story. There would be some amazing truths revealed over the next three to four months.

CHAPTER 8

Post Chetopa

Chapter 8

The week after the revival, a middle-aged woman who had attended our local meetings told me that she was approached in a restaurant, *in public*, and asked if she would like to join their coven of witches that meet weekly. Upon hearing this, I remembered that Angelique had said, "They are in every town and the leaders will usually be some of the top money people." The woman who approached our friend is a millionaire real estate broker. This real estate broker stated that they are just "white witches." By the term "white witch," she was referring to witches that use their power for themselves, and not against others. But often, their selfish desires impose on the lives and wills of others. There is nothing "white," clean, holy, acceptable or pure about any form of witchcraft. Furthermore, the earth is not your mother. Your mother is your mother. You were created in the image and likeness of God, the Father.

Angelique told us that those who work in the dark arts are well funded and are infiltrating churches through a new plan. She asked me if I had seen anyone slither down the aisle in church recently. She said, "The church eventually figured that out and stopped us from disrupting meetings. Now, witches just walk in. No more trying to shock or scare you. The plan is assimilation. We join the church, find the weak links and begin whispering in their ears. Conquer and divide."

About 1 month after the revival, a pastor who had heard pieces of Angelique's story, asked me if he could share it with a group of other pastors that he was going to be meeting with. I asked him not to, and said that I would prefer to come and share the story. You see to some, this might be a fantastic story, but to me…it's very personal, too important to miss any details, or to just skim through it. He was cautiously gracious. I said, "If you really want to talk to them, I'll do it with you." The Pastor agreed and said that he would send out invitations for pastors to come and sit in on this meeting.

Out of the fifty plus pastors invited, I found myself sitting with only 5 pastors and a few staff members of the hosting church. When I shared how Angelique had invested around 8 hours placing a curse on the city, and how she went through the names of the pastors, their families, elders of the churches, and leaders and officials of the town, one pastor's response stunned me. He said, "Well, that's why, whenever I drive by the city limits sign, I try to remember to bless my city."

A drive-by blessing? I'm sure his intentions were good, but is this what the church has come to? We have an enemy that will spend months finding out names, people and places, and then work to find the right curse, go out and spend a full night cursing the town, yet there are those among us that resort to a drive-by blessing!

I offered a solution. "Why don't you all get together, go out to the city limit signs, and bless and pray over the city?" They never did. In fact, after I had told this story, they opened the floor for discussion. It felt like every statement I had made was on trial. Each pastor was asked to share his thoughts about the events of Angelique's story. With a look of disbelief, some said nothing at all. One pastor kept saying, "I don't know what to say!" He looked a bit fearful. Another pastor was very angry because he felt we were giving the devil too much recognition. At one point, he said that it was like trying to find a demon behind every tree and under every rock.

At some point along the way, I had heard enough. I said to them, "It doesn't matter one rat's...what you think about it; this is exactly what they are doing, not only this one case, but in every city and every town, regardless the size of the community.

The pastor in charge of "the trial," closed with his recommendation to the others. "I recommend we just sit on this and not discuss this with any of our congregants. We don't need to start any trouble where none exists." In other words, "Don't rock the boat." They all agreed and never discussed the issue again to my knowledge.

Angelique had been responsible for closing down 3 churches in the area. Pastor Ray confirmed this to be true. (Angelique and I visited mostly by phone in the months following her conversion.) In one conversation, I asked Angelique how she had successfully closed 3 churches. Speaking in present tense of past events, this is what she said:

"I can walk into any church unchallenged. No one will say anything negative to me. Church people usually welcome me right into the fold. I could immediately see the spirits that were attached to the church people. For example, this guy has a spirit of lust and looks at porn all the time; that woman likes to drink; this guy is after that girl; I can see those spirits because I know them all."

Of all the spirits she interacted with, Angelique told me that the spirit she worked with most often, was the Spirit of Fear. She explained that he is not an emotion. He is a ruling spirit.

2 Timothy 1:7 (NKJV)
⁷ For God has not given us <u>a spirit of fear</u>, but of power and of love and of a sound mind.

Whether an educated society wishes to acknowledge it or not, there is a very real spiritual realm. There are angels and demons, light and darkness. Some individuals will acknowledge angels, light and heaven, but not demons, darkness and hell. But, darkness is very real.

Angelique asked us, "Have you ever seen a shadow out of the corner of your eye? You looked and swore that you had seen something there. You felt the hair on your neck stand on end? That's darkness. It's real. Darkness is a real thing and it can even move in the daytime. If you've experienced that, you most likely caught a glimpse of one of us moving. If you were sure you saw something, but when you turned, it was not there, Angelique restated, "That's us." (By "us" she meant witches moving by demonic power.)

"The second church I closed down was different. I observed the people on the stage singing before church. I could immediately see that the husband who led the singing kind of had a thing for a woman on stage that was not his wife. His wife seemed to be very insecure, and she kind of knew something was going on. I was immediately drawn to the wife. I asked myself, 'What's the most damage I can do to this place?' It was because I hated these people. I hated everything that had anything to do with God. So I placed a curse on the poor little wife that caused her to gain lots of weight. Over a period of time, I watched as I played on her worst fears of her husband wanting another woman. She began to gain weight, a whole bunch of weight, until her husband could not stand to look at her any more, and he eventually turned to the arms of his beautiful singer girl. They had an affair and it split the whole church. Within one year the church was closed down, and the wife became very ill."

"The third church I targeted, I entered without detection as well. How is it that I can walk into a church and see the spirits on all those people, but they can't see the spirits on me? I roll out of bed with no less than 6 demons every single day. I never leave the house without summoning 6 demons to be with me for my protection and to do my bidding. Other witches tried to kill me at times. Big mistake. I have a murderous spirit. He is fear. He is huge, ugly and scary, and he's mine. The last witch that tried to take me out found out really fast not to mess with me. She's dead now."

I asked her, "How did you kill her? How do you not get caught?" She said, "You'll never see me coming. I am clothed in darkness. I asked, "You are invisible?" "No, I'm clothed in darkness, and move only in the dark, so you will never see me coming." "So how did you kill her?" "The same way I killed everyone else except for my grandmother. I slit their throats and left."

"How and why did you kill your grandmother?"

"My father required me to kill his mother...my very own grandmother...as a test of my loyalty to the family. In this case, I gave her an overdose of drugs. She was elderly and sick already, so no one raised any questions. But you can't imagine what it did to my soul.

Angelique continued. "So I walked into this third church that I had been working on for some time when this sweet little old lady came to greet me at the back door like she had been waiting for me. She said, 'I know what you are doing here.' I said, 'Oh yeah? What are you going to do about it?' She said, 'I'm going to pray for you right now.' She came at me to touch me, and I said, 'Don't you touch me. Don't you touch me!' But, she did, and I immediately noticed she didn't have *The Spirit* so I gave her one of mine, and she lost her mind."

When I asked Pastor Ray about this story, he said, "All I know is this poor woman called me that Sunday night, screaming into the phone, 'Help me! Help me!' She lost her mind and is sitting down at the local nursing home, babbling like an idiot at this very moment."

Angelique continued, "Word got out about the old lady losing her mind. I continued going to that church and people got scared, as they should have, and eventually quit attending. They asked me to leave a few times, but I refused, telling them, 'Make me!' I could see the spirits on them, but they couldn't see the spirits on me.

She went in a triangle pattern to 3 different places around this town and worked up curses calling upon the names of gods that she had no idea were recorded in the Bible. At times, when working spells and pronouncing curses, Angelique would bring her children with her so that they could be part of that process.

When we were out there talking about the curses, she mentioned something very powerful. "You have to speak a curse. You have to say it out loud and you have to follow it to the 'T.' You don't get to do or say whatever you want and expect the curse to work. You have to follow the book of spells perfectly for it to work effectively."

This was interesting to me considering most Christians want to do whatever they want and say whatever they want, expecting the Bible to work for them. After this was all over, it was so cool to watch Angelique follow the Bible and see it work in her life. In the dark arts, Angelique had learned the discipline and principles of having what you say and saying exactly what you want. She learned the power of words spoken and the importance of following the book's "recipe." I wish Christians knew this. She was going to tell them with me. We were going to travel from church to church sharing her story. She was excited at the thought that after everything she had done to spite Him, that God would actually use her for His glory.

As we stood out at the edge of town by the river, she said, "I don't even have to curse this town anymore. The people do it for me by all the shit they say about this place and the people." Then she said, "We are well organized. We are well funded and it's not that we all like each other, because we don't, but an enemy of my enemy is my friend. We all come together for the destruction of the church and all things precious to God.

She talked about the power of being unified with others against the church, even mentioning ISIS and their role. She said, "I know every pastor's name. I know where they live and what church they pastor. I know the names of their wives, children and even their pets. Sometimes, I will kill a pet and leave it in some weird ritual looking way to scare them a little. It usually doesn't mean anything; I'm just trying to scare them, and it works every time."

"I know the names of all the deacons and church staff, and I curse them all. No one has ever stood against me. They all run in fear. One of my best weapons is something for which I don't have to exert any energy for—denial. They don't like to think that we exist. They don't believe in witches and spells because we have made them into cartoons and people flying on brooms and wearing a pointy hat." Jokingly, I asked, "Do you have a broom?" "No, I don't have a broom, but you better believe that I can fly! I can summon demons that can transport me where ever I need to go."

"My greatest weapon is the church's refusal to believe that we actually exist. The denial is so prevalent that we can walk right in to the doors of their churches. They seem so arrogant until they are challenged. We are taking this to their doorstep now. We aren't hiding anymore. We are coming to your town, your house, your church and bringing it to the doorstep of the churches. Greater is he that is in me than he that is in you!" (Speaking of the devil in her being greater.)

She said, "You are the first person in my entire life that I was not able to control, manipulate or defeat. And I see the true power of Jesus Christ. He really is greater, isn't He?"

She continued, "The churches' refusal to believe that we exist and that we have any power is exactly why the church is getting its ass whipped! They let us walk in and assume that just because we are attending, that we pose no threat or danger."

Angelique also shared with me how personal items would be taken from the person in which the curse would be placed upon. Hair, teeth, pictures...anything with DNA. Evil spirits are summoned like a hound dog sniffing a scent. They find the DNA match and the curse attaches itself inside a person's body. There is a great need for believers to understand the implications of being a New Creature in Christ Jesus! We actual receiving new DNA, i.e., the Divine Nature of the Almighty within our human spirit. Ignorance and denial opens the door to the enemy.

Hosea 4:6 KJV

6 My people are destroyed for lack of knowledge: because thou hast rejected knowledge, I will also reject thee, that thou shalt be no priest to me: seeing thou hast forgotten the law of thy God, I will also forget thy children.

CHAPTER 9

Back Home

Chapter 9

By Kirk DeMars

After we left Chetopa and returned to our home, we were on a high from the trip but ready to get refreshed and rested. I think because we were so fatigued, we weren't quite ready for what happened that first night home.

My wife and I were sitting on the couch, unwinding and watching a DVD when she began to get this overwhelming feeling that something was very wrong. Suddenly, she felt like she was dying. We took action right away.

As we began praying, the Holy Spirit revealed to her that she had made a point of contact. What I mean by a point of contact is, that while we were in Chetopa, my wife had wanted to love on Angelique by giving her a bottle of perfume that she had. It was given with the intent to show her that she loved her. The Holy Spirit revealed to my wife that by giving that perfume bottle to her, she had given the enemy something to latch onto concerning my wife. Where that came into effect was that when she was thinking about giving the perfume, she wanted to do it out of compassion and love, but she felt like she shouldn't give it to her. Fighting with that thought, she gave it anyway because she didn't want to be selfish and wanted to be generous. Looking back on it, we believe the Holy Spirit was warning, "Don't give her that!"

Witches use many different things to try to establish footing on the curses that they place on people. Demons also scout for any possible connection or entry point. We believe now that there was a warning not to give that to her, but we did. So, after that was revealed, we got on the phone with Don, and we began praying together. We broke that curse that was spoken over my wife and immediately, the heaviness left her! It was remarkable how quickly it all came on, but even more remarkable how quickly it left when it had been found out and told to leave.

Over the next few months, I had many phone conversations with Angelique and her oldest son. Many times, Angelique was struggling with the evil that was constantly around her. The same thing was happening with her son. I can remember talking to him on a few different occasions. It would always a good conversation. He never seemed to waver from knowing that there was a change that happened in him when he accepted Christ as his Savior, but you could tell by his voice that he was weary. I prayed with him and encouraged him to keep moving forward in his new found hope. I always made sure to tell him that I loved him. He would tell me that he loved me, we would hang up and there would be a short period of time until our next conversation. We would pick right up where we left off. I believe that God had opened a door for me to find favor with this young man and just minister the love of the Father to him. There were times that I could tell that the evil was harassing him and causing him great turmoil and the only thing I could do was continue to love him through the phone. It was hard knowing that these kids were living with people who still practiced witchcraft.

My conversations with Angelique were always much more lively. She was in a constant struggle for her life. She told us so many different things that were going on and the daily struggle she was having with her family. She mentioned that she had fights with her sister, and that many times, the strife was a sneak attack on her. One time in particular, she told us that she had been drugged and then kidnapped by family members. The purpose of this kidnapping was that the witches she used to hang out with wanted to summon the demons through her again. They had lost their power and their foothold and they wanted it back! Angelique told us that through the drugs and her weakness, they were able to summon them again. I know this to be true because there were several conversations or text messages from her in which it was the demonic activity was obvious. However, through all of that, Angelique continued to want to live as a "New Creation." That is why we had so many conversations with her. She had found perfect love and she couldn't be separated from Jesus. Many of our conversations were just to reassure her that she was going to be okay and to remind her to read God's Word, which she kept trying to do. On a side note, it was neat to hear how the Holy Spirit was revealing things to her through the Word of God.

I can remember being at a high school football game with Don and his family, watching their oldest son play. While we were watching the game, I received a phone call from Angelique. She was very agitated. She was adamant that she had lost the baptism of the Holy Spirit with the evidence of speaking in tongues. I told her that was a lie from the enemy and that the Holy Spirit had not left her. She refused to believe that and I could tell that there was an outside force attacking her. It turned out, one of the people who had been trying to minister to her, was also tearing her down and was with her right at that moment. I told Angelique to get that person on the phone. This person proceeded to tell me how things weren't good with Angelique and that the demons were on her again. She went on and on about how things weren't good with her. She was saying this right in front of Angelique! I told the friend that I wanted to pray and then encouraged her to only speak life into Angelique. Angelique got back on the phone and continued with the "I lost it" mentality. I told her that we needed to take just a few moments to repent of anything we opened the door for and then we were going to pray in the Spirit together. She didn't think it would work, but she agreed. After we prayed, I told her I was going to start praying in the Spirit and then I wanted her to join me. It took quite a while and of course it was a little distracting for me with all of the game noise around me. I tried to find the quietest spot possible and then it happened. She started praying in tongues again. I think she was able to push through the lies to find the truth again. She *knew* what she experienced was real; she just needed to fight for it.

In other conversations, I encouraged her to keep praying in the Spirit and she did so. The enemy was angry and constantly attacked her. Our conversations continued throughout those few months after Chetopa.

In December of that same year, we had the Fourteen12 Winter Summit in Laurie, Missouri. Don and I talked frequently about whether Angelique would be able to attend and how great it would be if she could. Someone was able to bring her to the

Summit on a Thursday night and it was really good to see her. Angelique was already being tormented and had awful pain in her stomach which required prayer before the service even began. I remember some people were praying for her in the back of the room, and I went over to join in. I laid my right hand on her back and that is when I experienced something that I couldn't have dreamed up. When I laid my hand on her back, I felt a growl run right under my hand. I still look back on that event and think about how I would have reacted before I started really understanding my identity in Christ. I grew up watching a bunch of junk that bred fear into me. However, many years ago, that hold of fear was broken off of me. I confidently stood there with my hand on her back without fear, and commanded that thing to get out, and it obeyed me.

Angelique continued to have struggles during those last few days of the Winter Summit. There were numerous prayers and words of encouragement to help her. The people that were gathered at the Summit really took great responsibility in ministering to her. Many people gave money and gifts to bless Angelique and her kids with Christmas gifts. She seemed to be overwhelmed with the generosity and kept saying, "Why are these people being so nice to me? They don't even know me."

During her time there, Angelique was staying at a hotel and had numerous battles with the demonic. She was absolutely under attack. She kept telling us that they (the family) knew she was there, and they were coming to get her. She was able to make it through all of that, but there were some peculiar things that happened throughout that week.

One night while sitting outside of the venue, she said she heard someone call out her name before entering the bar next door. She expressed these word: "That freaked me out!" It was evident the devil was coming after her with everything that he had. Finally, the Summit ended and Angelique went back home. She didn't want to go, but she had to.

I began receiving some peculiar texts from her when she arrived home that was sadly very telling on the environment she was going back to. The text said, "You should not have let her come back. She's mine!" Disturbed by that, I sent a text back to find out what was going on. She sent back, "She's mine!" Along with that, there were other disturbing messages from this thing that was after her and speaking through her. It was disturbing because I knew that she was under attack from the very people that she called family. She had told us about the time after she got saved that her family kidnapped her by drugging her. During that time, we were trying to get in touch with her, but there were several days without any contact. She finally responded by telling us that while in an altered state, the family once again used her as a portal to summon demons.

We found later, that this same thing was apparently happening again after she returned to her home from the Winter Summit. There was a period of time when we didn't heard from her again.

After numerous attempts by Don and a few others, Angelique's mom responded cold-heartedly saying that Angelique was dead. We didn't believe this report because we knew that they didn't like us having contact with her. Don and I continued to pursue the truth on whether or not this had happened. I made numerous phone calls and got in touch with the Joplin Sheriff's department and was told that they couldn't give out that kind of information. After prayer and the leading of the Holy Spirit, I decided to call the coroner. The coroner returned my phone call and confirmed that Angelique was indeed dead. I asked him how it happened and he said that they found her lying face down. She had died from an apparent drug overdose. The coroner did not say anything more than that, but I could tell he knew that it was more than just an overdose. Don spoke with the coroner later in the week and he confirmed that she had been "highly medicated." When Don asked if she overdosed, the coroner answered again, "She was highly medicated." To us, he seemed to be indicating that she did not overdose. We believe that Angelique was again drugged by her family to help them summon the evil beings that they had so frequently called up before. This time, she was not able to handle the drugs. Her body had finally failed her from all of the drug abuse. Angelique Burwick was a friend of mine, and I am looking forward to the day when I get to see her in heaven. While we were sad at her passing, we were also thankful that she was now safe and secure in her loving Father's protection. A woman who had only known evil is now face to face with Perfect Love! I can only imagine that moment when she first set her eternal eyes upon Jesus. What a happy and joyous moment that must have been! Her earthly life has ended, but her story will go on to inspire millions to love people like Christ loved us. The message from our God and our Savior Jesus is that they don't want anyone to perish, but everyone to come to everlasting life!

CHAPTER 10

Conclusion

Chapter 10

So much of this account raises the question, "Can a Christian have a demon?" A true born-again Christian cannot be fully possessed...spirit, soul and body. But consider this. You live in a house. If your house has termites, no one would say that "you" have termites, but rather that your house does. You would simply call a termite exterminator. Your body is your earth suit...or your earthly *house*. The enemy could oppress your mind and emotions or actually take up residence in your body. This is often the case with certain disorders and diseases.

Luke 13:10-17 NKJV

A Spirit of Infirmity

10 Now He was teaching in one of the synagogues on the Sabbath. 11 And behold, there was a woman who had a spirit of infirmity eighteen years, and was bent over and could in no way raise herself up. 12 But when Jesus saw her, He called her to Him and said to her, "Woman, you are loosed from your infirmity." 13 And He laid His hands on her, and immediately she was made straight, and glorified God.

14 But the ruler of the synagogue answered with indignation, because Jesus had healed on the Sabbath; and he said to the crowd, "There are six days on which men ought to work; therefore come and be healed on them, and not on the Sabbath day."

15 The Lord then answered him and said, "Hypocrite![a] Does not each one of you on the Sabbath loose his ox or donkey from the stall, and lead it away to water it? 16 So ought not this woman, being a daughter of Abraham, whom Satan has bound—think of it—for eighteen years, be loosed from this bond on the Sabbath?" 17 And when He said these things, all His adversaries were put to shame; and all the multitude rejoiced for all the glorious things that were done by Him.

It should also be very apparent from this true account of our experience with Angelique, that the enemy is manifesting supernatural signs today. He has no creative ability, so he endeavors to mimic God's supernatural ability.

God has given to the church, the nine supernatural gifts of the Spirit. Too much of the Church has explained these biblical phenomena as natural abilities...but they are not. Our insistence on emasculating First Corinthians Chapter Twelve has had tragic results. We are created to walk in power and authority with the ability to do the works of Jesus.

John 14:12 KJV
12 Verily, verily, I say unto you, He that believeth on me, the works that I do shall he do also; and greater works than these shall he do; because I go unto my Father.

Mankind knows that there is more than what can be experienced through the physical senses. We subconsciously hunger for what belongs to us. Ignorance of the Spiritual gifts in the Word of God, as well as the rebellious refusal to acknowledge anything beyond one's present experience, has resulted in a power void; hence, multitudes are drawn away by lying signs and wonders. This is clearly demonstrated in the Harry Potter series, and even more so in the Vampire Romance Story...the Twilight Saga, Breaking Dawn...in which the enemy mimics the ability to see and know present and future things through supernatural ability which rightfully belongs to the Church. The enemy shares his power with people...but always at a costly price not revealed presently to them. The Holy Spirit shares His power and insight with the Church to help hurting, broken people and to impart lasting joy. There is no cost, but rather great reward in this life and the next which results from yielding to the Holy Spirit of God.

Deuteronomy 18:9-14 ESV

Abominable Practices

⁹ "When you come into the land that the LORD your God is giving you, you shall not learn to follow the abominable practices of those nations. ¹⁰ There shall not be found among you anyone who burns his son or his daughter as an offering,[a] anyone who practices divination or tells fortunes or interprets omens, or a sorcerer ¹¹ or a charmer or a medium or a necromancer or one who inquires of the dead, ¹² for whoever does these things is an abomination to the LORD. And because of these abominations the LORD your God is driving them out before you. ¹³ You shall be blameless before the LORD your God, ¹⁴ for these nations, which you are about to dispossess, listen to fortune-tellers and to diviners. But as for you, the LORD your God has not allowed you to do this.

The following are forbidden Occult Practices: Human Sacrifice, Divination, Astrology, Enchantments, Witchcraft and Witches (including "white witches"), Charmers, Consulters with Familiar Spirits, Wizards, and Necromancers. Shape shifting also springs from Darkness.

1Human Sacrifice – Abortion is one example
2) Divination – Demonic Manipulation
3) Astrology – Worshiping the stars; zodiac
4) Enchanter – Someone satanically endowed to produce seductive spells.
5) Witchcraft and Witches – Includes its modern, organized counterpart, Wicca.
6) Charmer – One who manipulates objects or beings via demonic power.
7) Consulter with Familiar Spirits – One who gleans knowledge from demonic contact.
8) Wizards – Practitioners of magical arts
9) Necromancers – Those who claim to be in contact with the dead.

Isaiah 47:12-15 ESV

Stand fast in your enchantments and your many sorceries, with which you have labored from your youth; perhaps you may be able to succeed; perhaps you may inspire terror. You are wearied with your many counsels; let them stand forth and save you, those who divide the heavens, who gaze at the stars, who at the new moons make known what shall come upon you. Behold, they are like stubble; the fire consumes them; they cannot deliver themselves from the power of the flame. No coal for warming oneself is this, no fire to sit before! Such to you are those with whom you have labored, who have done business with you from your youth; they wander about, each in his own direction; there is no one to save you.

Zechariah 10:2 ESV

For the household gods utter nonsense, and the diviners see lies; they tell false dreams and give empty consolation. Therefore the people wander like sheep; they are afflicted for lack of a shepherd.

Ezekiel 12:24 ESV

For there shall be no more any false vision or flattering divination within the house of Israel.

2 Chronicles 33:6 ESV

And he burned his sons as an offering in the Valley of the Son of Hinnom, and used fortune-telling and omens and sorcery, and dealt with mediums and with necromancers. He did much evil in the sight of the Lord, provoking him to anger.

1 Samuel 15:23 ESV

For rebellion is as the sin of divination, and presumption is as iniquity and idolatry. Because you have rejected the word of the Lord, he has also rejected you from being king."

Leviticus 20:6 ESV

"If a person turns to mediums and necromancers, whoring after them, I will set my face against that person and will cut him off from among his people.

If you crave power, but have pursued the dark arts, you are missing your destiny.

Jeremiah 29:11-13 Amplified

[11] For I know the plans and thoughts that I have for you,' says the LORD, 'plans for peace and well-being and not for disaster to give you a future and a hope. [12] Then you will call on Me and you will come and pray to Me, and I will hear [your voice] and I will listen to you. [13] Then [with a deep longing] you will seek Me and require Me [as a vital necessity] and [you will] find Me when you search for Me with all your heart.

God created you. God loves you. God has a good plan for you. He wants to be your very own Father. He is not responsible for any of the bad things that have befallen you in life.

Jeremiah 29:11-13 NIV

Everyone who calls on the name of the Lord [Jesus] will be saved.

Your Heavenly Father has been waiting patiently for you. Don't put this off for another moment. Right now, say these words aloud and let your heart agree:

> Dear God in heaven, I come to you in the name of Jesus. I believe that your Son Jesus Christ shed His precious blood on the cross and died for my sins. You said in Romans 10:9 that if we confess that Jesus is Lord, we shall be saved.

Right now I confess Jesus as the Lord of my soul. With my heart, I believe that God raised Jesus from the dead. This very moment I accept Jesus Christ as my own personal Savior and according to His Word, right now I am saved.

Thank you Jesus for your unlimited grace which has saved me from my sins. Therefore Lord Jesus transform my life so that I may bring glory and honor to you alone and not to myself. Set me free from all demon power right now in Jesus Name. Thank you Jesus for dying for me and giving me eternal life. Amen.

About the Author

Television and radio host, author and evangelist, Don Allen continues on the front lines of world evangelism. For over 10 years now, he has embarked upon the advancement of the cause for Christ, traveling internationally to nations including Ethiopia, Malawi, El-Salvador, and throughout the United States.

He believes that the Gospel works in every culture, in the midst of every religion and in this generation. He continues the quest to manifest to this generation, the miracle ministry of Jesus Christ.

Don is earnestly contending for the faith that was once delivered to the saints. His mission is two-fold. First, he wants to help you position yourself to receive your miracle…your healing. Second, he wants to teach you how to go and bring this healing power of God to the lost and dying world, and convince them that there is still a God in heaven that loves them.

Don Allen began by teaching a Prayer and Healing school in 2000. Through study of the scriptures, he began to uncover the modern day miracle ministry of Jesus Christ. He began to see that Bible methods still produce Bible results.

Don currently holds weekly meetings at The Christ the Healer Studio in Laurie, MO, The Missouri State Capitol in Jefferson City, MO, and in Kona, Hawaii and operates a Prayer Room in Versailles, MO. Don Allen is the host of "Christ the Healer" television show. He also has a Miracle and Healing room in Ethiopia, where local evangelists pray for the sick and have seen many miracles. Over the past 10 years, there have been many documented miracles in this ministry, as they have taught people how to stand on and believe the Word of God. Don presses on passionately, driven by the worldwide heart-cry for the love and miracle ministry of Jesus Christ.

For more information, go to our website at www.twoguysandabible.com.

Be on the lookout for my new book—**Binding the Strongman**—COMING SOON!

$9.99
ISBN 978-0-9984544-0-5
50999>